Best Friends Never Give Up

A true story

Written by Alayne McKee, illustrated by Carol Green

We hope you enjoy our story
Alayne + Tia

Published by Gillian A. McKee, Aotearoa New Zealand.

Text © 2021 Alayne McKee, Illustrations © 2021 Carol Green.

ISBN 978-0-473-58394-1

Look across Manukau Harbour and you might see a ten-year-old chocolate Labrador called Tia and her best friend Alayne. Every day they walk around their friendly little village, along the harbour's edge and past the farm.

They stop and chat to all the dogs they meet—and the people too of course. They even say "kia ora!" to the little kitten up the road. He's a bit unpredictable—sometimes he's friendly and smoochy but at other times he puffs out his fur and swipes at them with his paw.

I'll tell you a secret... Tia may be a dog, but she is a scaredy-*cat!*

She's a little bit afraid of that kitten.

One day they decided to go on holiday. They rented a bach, packed up the car and started the long drive. Alayne listened to the radio and Tia slept. Tia sleeps a lot! In fact, she spends most of her time sleeping, eating, or persuading people to scratch her bum!

Halfway through their journey they stopped at a café and Alayne bought a toasted sandwich to share with Tia. Now, Tia is not usually allowed toasted sandwiches, but they were on holiday, so this was a special occasion. And Tia does *love* ham, cheese, and pineapple toasted sandwiches.

After lunch, they set off again and a few hours later they arrived at the bach deep in the countryside. *Mīharo!* It was the perfect place for a holiday. There was an enormous garden with tall trees, pretty flowers, a rope swing, a henhouse and another bach.

A lovely couple called Peter and Jane were staying in the other bach with Charlie their adorable puppy. Charlie bounded over to welcome Tia and the two dogs became good friends.

Now it was time for Tia to explore the garden. Off she went sniffing every blade of grass and following every scent. *Sniff, sniff, sniff.* In fact, she sniffed her way across the garden until she came to a lake.

Labradors love water, and they are usually very good at swimming. But not Tia, she hates swimming because she doesn't like getting her face wet. However, she loves paddling especially if the water is muddy and stinky. The *stinkier* the better!

Tia was disappointed that this lake wasn't muddy or stinky, but she was thirsty, and the water smelled fresh, so she plunged in for a drink. *Ahhhhh!*

Before long Tia was back on the scent and this time, she followed her nose right up to a fence. She had been concentrating so much that she almost bumped into it! She looked up and saw two sets of big yellow eyes staring down at her.

Taihoa! Tia stood completely still, except for her nose which was working overtime. She had caught a whiff of one of her favourite things... *rabbit poo!* You will not be surprised to hear that she spent the rest of the afternoon eating all the rabbit poo she could find. Alayne thinks it is a disgusting habit, but Tia doesn't care.

That night, Alayne and Tia were tired after their long journey. As Tia lay sleeping her legs moved, her tail wagged and she made strange, muffled barking sounds *Mmmwuff, Mmmwuff.* Alayne wondered if Tia was dreaming about chasing rabbits.

What do you think she was dreaming about?

The next morning Tia woke up early. Alayne was still asleep, but Tia was hungry, so she wanted Alayne to wake up.

Most dogs whine or bark when they want to get someone's attention but not Tia. When she wants to get attention, she politely shakes her head from side to side so that her ears flap. *Flappity flap, flappity, flap!*

So, Tia stood outside the bedroom door and flapped her ears.

It worked! Alayne woke up and gave Tia her breakfast.

"Ka pai!" Tia quietly congratulated herself for training Alayne so well.

Tia ate her breakfast in about five seconds. *1, 2, 3, 4, 5, gone!* Then she went outside for a look around. Charlie joined her and the two friends wandered down the garden wagging their tails and sniffing the grass.

A few minutes later Charlie came back on his own, so Alayne went to find Tia. She walked round the garden, twice, but could not see her. Alayne called, but Tia did not come.

Alayne was puzzled. Where could she be? Alayne went to see Peter and Jane.

"Have you seen Tia?" she asked.

"No, we haven't seen her," they replied.

Peter and Jane knew that Alayne was worried, so they searched the garden too.
They even clambered over the giant compost heap at the bottom of the garden.
Hidden behind the compost heap they found a small hole in the fence. "Could Tia
have squeezed through that hole?" they asked doubtfully.

They hiked through *all* the fields surrounding the garden and they rowed around the lake. They looked everywhere. They called *"Tia, Tia!"* but Tia did not come.

Peter and Jane asked all the neighbours if they had seen Tia. No one had seen her. *Tia had disappeared!*

Friends and neighbours joined the search. They sent photos of Tia to everyone they knew and asked people to look out for her.

It was a mystery. The facts were clear:

1. Tia was not in the garden.

2. The garden was surrounded by fences.

3. Dogs do not vanish into thin air.

Auē! That just left the lake. Could Tia have gone into the lake?

Have you seen Tia?
She went missing on Tuesday.
She is friendly and gentle and probably VERY HUNGRY.

Alayne didn't know what to think or where to look. She phoned some friends and told them the awful news that Tia was missing.

OH NO! I HOPE YOU FIND HER SOON!

Alayne couldn't sleep that night. She kept thinking about Tia. The same thoughts kept going around and around in her head. What had happened to Tia? Was she lost? Was she hurt? Would Alayne ever see her again?

But Alayne also thought about the hole in the fence. Did Tia squeeze through? Had she gone on an adventure?

At dawn the next morning, Alayne went outside to search for Tia again. She looked in the lake. She checked the garden. There was no sign of Tia. She investigated the hole in the fence. "Maybe Tia did squeeze through that hole," she said to herself.

Alayne looked in the field behind the compost heap. She called Tia, but Tia did not come. Alayne felt miserable. She did not think she would ever see Tia again. She even wondered if she should just give up and go home.

WEDNESDAY

What do you think Alayne should do?

But wait! Some neighbours came to see Alayne. They had a *clue*. Someone had seen an old chocolate Labrador walking down Rata Road about six kilometres away. Maybe it was Tia?

"Don't give up. Let's keep looking. We'll all help," said the neighbours.

Alayne and the neighbours made a plan:

- Some of them would drive around and put flyers in mailboxes, cafés, and on community noticeboards.

- Some of them would contact all the vets and the SPCA to ask if anyone had found Tia.

- Some of them would keep searching for Tia.

DO YOU HAVE ANY OTHER IDEAS?

Alayne drove to Rata Road. She talked to everyone she met, and gave them a flyer, and asked if they had seen Tia. Everyone was very kind, but no one had seen Tia.

Alayne drove back to the bach and told everyone the bad news. She had found the chocolate Labrador, but it wasn't Tia. Nobody had seen Tia.

Alayne did not know what else to do. So, everyone searched the garden again. They looked in the lake. They investigated the hole in the fence, and they walked through the field behind the compost heap. They drove up and down country roads. They drove through orchards. There was still no sign of Tia.

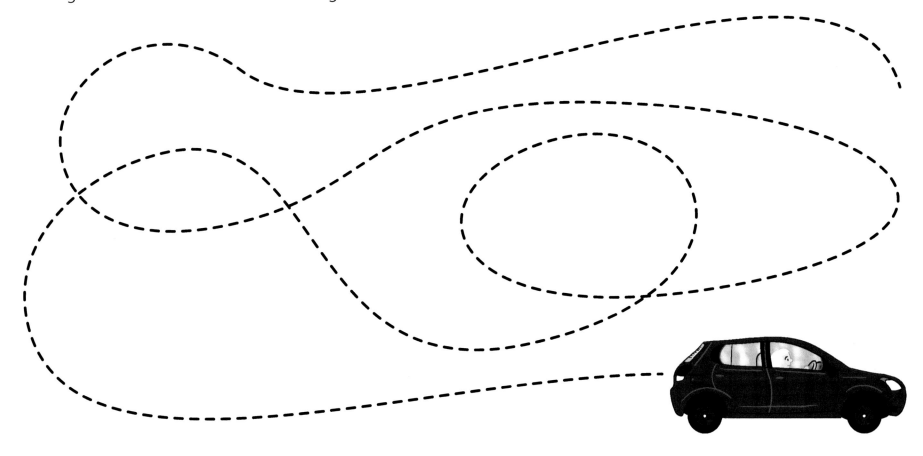

There were no more clues. Everyone had looked everywhere they could think of. Alayne was so sad. She thought she would never see Tia again so she told everyone that she would drive home the next day.

That night, Alayne was full to the brim with all sorts of feelings.

Have you ever felt like that?

She really missed having her furry friend curled up beside her. Alayne's friends tried to make her feel better.

The next morning, Alayne went to look for Tia *for the last time*. She didn't think that she would find Tia, but she looked anyway. She looked in the garden. She searched the lake. There was still no sign of Tia.

Alayne trudged through the field behind the compost heap. She called *"Tia… Tia!"* Suddenly… Alayne heard some howling.

"Aoooooo! Aoooooo!"

Alayne thought she was imagining things. She called *"Tia!"* again.

"Aoooooo! Aoooooo!"

Alayne could not believe it! It was Tia! She ran towards the howling, but she couldn't see Tia anywhere. All she could see was grass. It was as if the field was howling.

Alayne needed help so she ran to Peter and Jane's house. *"I found Tia. She's alive. She's in the field. Please come!"* she called breathlessly.

Peter and Jane got dressed and came running to help her. Alayne called *"Tia!"*

"Aoooooo! Aoooooo! Aoooooo! Aoooooo!"

Alayne, Peter, and Jane ran towards the howling but there was no sign of Tia. They kept moving closer and closer towards the howling until it sounded like they were standing right on top of it. They looked down, and through the dense long grass they saw two eyes and a wet nose.

Tia had fallen into a *sinkhole!* Peter reached down and with a colossal heave he hauled Tia out.

Tia was ecstatic! She bounced around licking everyone and jumping up on them. She was so excited she nearly bounced right back into the sinkhole!

Ka mau te wehi! Everyone was delighted. *Tia was alive!* She was very dirty and a bit wet, but she wasn't hurt!

Back at the bach they made cups of tea, and Tia needed her breakfast. Labradors are *always* hungry, and Tia had not eaten for two days, so she wasn't just hungry, she was *ravenous*.

After breakfast Tia lay on her bed and fell asleep. She was exhausted and she slept for hours and hours.

Alayne sat beside Tia stroking her soft fur and watching her sleeping. She tried to imagine how Tia had felt when she was stuck in the sinkhole. Was she scared? Was she cold? Had she thought about Alayne?

Perhaps she had not thought about anything at all.

Alayne, Peter and Jane spread the happy news that Tia had been found. They thanked everyone who had been so kind and so helpful.

Alayne knew she could not have rescued Tia without everyone's help. She would have given up much too soon. Alayne's friends and all the lovely people who helped her had given her hope and encouraged her to keep looking.

The next morning, Tia and Alayne packed the car and drove home.

They had not had much fun on their holiday, but they did have an adventure. And do you know what?

Tia's ready for another one!

GO

LNT1A

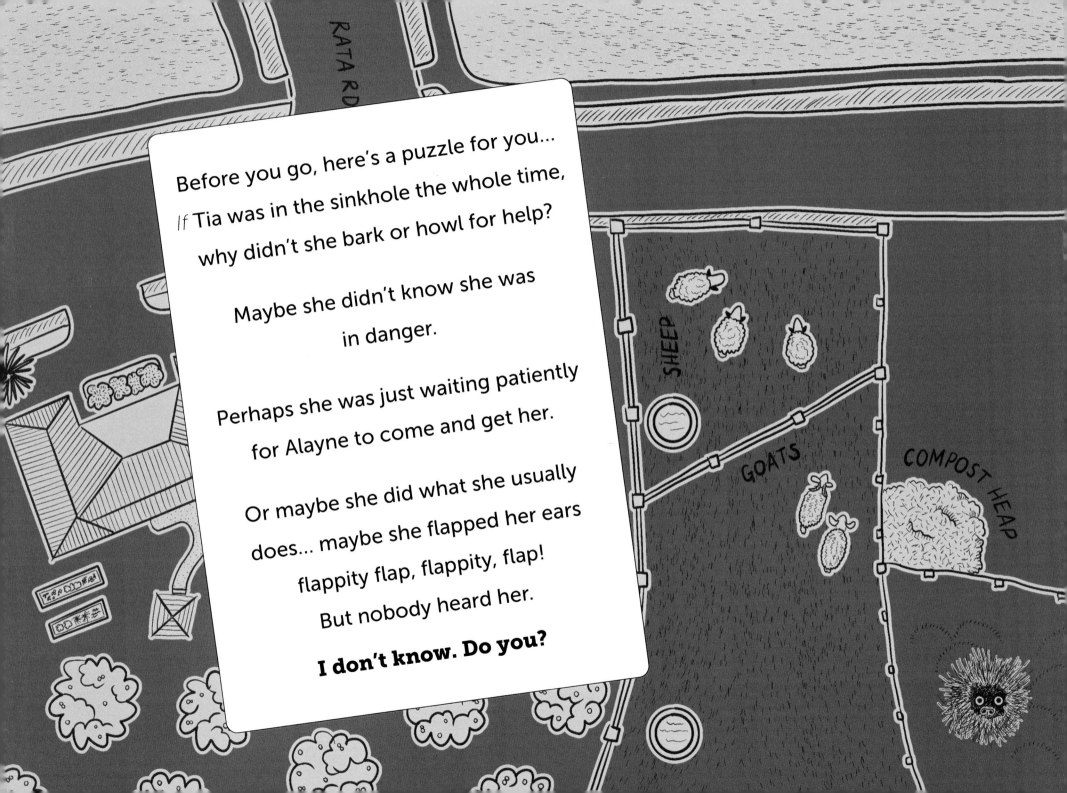

Before you go, here's a puzzle for you...
If Tia was in the sinkhole the whole time,
why didn't she bark or howl for help?

Maybe she didn't know she was
in danger.

Perhaps she was just waiting patiently
for Alayne to come and get her.

Or maybe she did what she usually
does... maybe she flapped her ears
flappity flap, flappity, flap!
But nobody heard her.

I don't know. Do you?

For my nephew Patrick who made me read stories until my voice was hoarse

and for my niece Izabella who loves reading as much as I do.

And for the wonderful community in a beautiful part of Aotearoa New Zealand

who searched for Tia, and looked after Alayne. Thank you!

Interesting words and phrases for international readers

Kia ora! Hello! Cheers! Good luck! Best wishes!

Mīharo Marvellous, amazing

Bach A small house or weekend cottage

Taihoa By and by, wait, don't...yet

Ka pai Good

Auē Heck! Oh dear!

Kia kaha Be strong, get stuck in, keep going

Aroha nui e hoa Much love/with deep affection my friend

Ka mau te wehi! How terrible! How terrific! Fantastic! Awesome!

Definitions from maoridictionary.co.nz and www.merriam-webster.com

THE BACH

THE FIELD

GATE

THE LAKE